Oceanography
by *Edward P. Ortleb and Richard Cadice*

This book presents a program of basic studies dealing with the science of oceanography. Various characteristics of the oceans are described, including features of the oceans, life within the oceans, and different ways of studying the oceans.

Each of the twelve teaching units in this book is introduced by a color mini poster, which emphasizes the basic concept of the unit and presents questions for discussion. Reproducible student pages provide reinforcement and follow-up activities.

The teaching guide offers descriptions of the basic concepts to be presented, background information, suggestions for enrichment activities, and a complete answer key.

Artist: Donald O'Connor
Managing Editor: Kathleen Hilmes

Copyright © 1991
Milliken Publishing Company
a Lorenz company
P.O. Box 802
Dayton, OH 45401-0802
www.LorenzEducationalPress.com

Permission to reproduce pages extends only to teacher-purchaser for individual classroom use, not to exceed in any event more than one copy per pupil in a course. The reproduction of any part for an entire school or school system or for commercial use is strictly prohibited.

CONTENTS

* Full-color mini posters are found at the back of the book.
Each poster should be used to introduce the corresponding unit.

TEACHING GUIDE

Page 1 OCEANS AND THE SEAS OF THE WORLD

CONCEPTS: 1. All oceans of the world are part of one vast body of water. 2. Nearly three-fourths of the earth's surface is covered by water.

BACKGROUND INFORMATION: There are no dividing lines between the five great oceans of the world. Each ocean is connected with at least two others. The five great oceans according to size are the Pacific, Atlantic, Indian, Southern, and the Arctic. The Southern, a continuous belt of water surrounding the South Pole land mass, is sometimes regarded as a southern extension of the Atlantic, Pacific, and Indian Oceans. The Pacific Ocean, the largest and deepest, has an average depth of 4280 meters. It covers nearly 37% of the total area of the world ocean. The Atlantic is the second largest in size and depth. The average depth of the Atlantic is 4270 meters. It covers almost 25% of the total area of the world ocean. The Indian Ocean is the third largest in size and has an average depth of 3960 meters. It covers about 12% of the total area of the world ocean. The Arctic, often considered a northern extension of the Atlantic, has an average depth of 1280 meters. Much of this ocean is completely covered with ice to a depth of 2.5 to 3 meters. In summer months, some of the ice breaks up into drifting sections called floes. The Arctic Ocean covers about 3% of the total area of the world ocean.

Oceanographers use the term sea to denote divisions of ocean water near land. There are many seas on this planet and they are usually classified into two divisions: enclosed and partly enclosed. An enclosed sea penetrates deeply into a large land mass and is connected with the open ocean by a narrow passage. A partly enclosed sea is linked with the open ocean by a wide passageway. The largest sea in area is the Coral Sea. It has an average depth of about 2471 meters. The South China Sea is second largest in area with an average depth of 1180 meters. Next, according to area, are the Caribbean Sea, Bering Sea, Mediterranean Sea, the Sea of Okhotsk, and the Gulf of Mexico. The Sea of Okhotsk has an average depth of 814 meters. In comparing ocean and sea depths, the Sea of Okhotsk is relatively shallow.

ENRICHMENT ACTIVITIES: 1. Find out about Project Mohole. 2. Find out about the work and lives of ocean explorers Vasco da Gama and James Cook.

ANSWER KEY:

Page 1 1. The oceans from largest to smallest area are the Pacific, Atlantic, Indian, Southern, and Arctic. The seas from largest to smallest area are the Coral Sea, South China Sea, Caribbean Sea, Bering Sea, Mediterranean Sea, Sea of Okhotsk, and the Gulf of Mexico. 2. The great oceans are really parts of one continuous body of water as can be seen when you turn a globe upside down and around. **Study Question:** It takes longer for the sun to heat the ocean than the land because water changes temperature more slowly than air or land masses. The slowness of water to change temperature and the vastness of the water on the earth's surface help explain how the climate of the planet is controlled by the ocean. The ocean keeps the air from becoming too cold or too hot; the ocean is also an important part of the water cycle on this planet.

Page 1a 1. A. Arctic Ocean B. Bering Sea C. Gulf of Mexico D. Caribbean Sea E. Atlantic Ocean F. Pacific Ocean G. North Sea H. Mediterranean Sea I. Black Sea J. Sea of Japan K. Yellow Sea L. South China Sea M. Arabian Sea N. Tasman Sea O. Indian Ocean P. Southern Ocean 2. Circle Gulf of Mexico and Caribbean Sea 3a. warm, poles b. Tasman Sea, Australia c. Arctic, southernmost d. Mediterranean Sea e. Pacific, five 4a. Atlantic Ocean b. Indian Ocean c. Mediterranean Sea d. Yellow Sea e. Bering Sea 5. Salt water has a greater density than freshwater; therefore, a swimmer can float and swim with greater ease in ocean water.

Page 2 MAJOR OCEAN CURRENTS

CONCEPTS: 1. The waters of the oceans and seas are constantly moving in currents. 2. Each major ocean has a predominant current flowing within it.

BACKGROUND INFORMATION: Long ago sailors realized that there were "rivers" in the oceans. They were experiencing currents. Currents are primarily caused by the force of winds blowing on the water. Several factors affect the directional flow of currents. One factor is heat from the sun. When equatorial waters become heated, they expand and flow toward the poles. The colder polar waters sink and flow toward the equator near the ocean floor. This produces a continuous movement of water. In addition to the sun's heat, the earth's rotation affects ocean currents. The earth rotates at 1600 km an hour at the equator. Since the spin is eastward, the waters tend to move clockwise in the Northern Hemisphere, and counterclockwise in the Southern Hemisphere. Wind is a third factor that affects ocean currents. On earth, different winds blow with different velocities and from different directions. From the east, within the tropics, come the trade winds; from the west, in high latitudes, come the westerlies. These circulating winds tend to push the surface waters in different directions. Continental land is yet another factor affecting ocean currents. The outlines of the earth's large land masses (continents) cause the currents to turn and change direction.

In some years, a current can change course; it can also carry less water if the wind does not blow as hard. Currents do affect the climates of their neighboring regions. The Gulf Stream, which affects Florida's climate, is an example. The Gulf Stream is a very strong current. It is about 160 km wide and travels approximately 6.4 km per hour. The Gulf Stream branches into other currents – Labrador Current, North Atlantic Current, and the Canary Current. All of these currents together form a complete circle. The Pacific Ocean north of the equator has the counterpart of the Gulf Stream, called the Kuroshio Current. This current branches into the Alaskan Current, California Current, and the North Equatorial Current.

The South Equatorial Currents, chiefly the Brazil and Benguela currents, are similar to the flow of the North Equatorial Currents except in direction. The South Equatorial Current moves westward across the Pacific Ocean. It includes the Humboldt Current. The current carries cold water from the South Pole along the South American coast and then rejoins the South Equatorial Current of the Pacific. Westerly winds produce the West Wind Drift Current in the Southern Ocean. It completely circles the Antarctic region because there are no land masses in the area.

ENRICHMENT ACTIVITIES: Find out about the Sargasso Sea. 2. Research the Coriolis Effect.

ANSWER KEY:
Page 2 1. Currents north of the equator flow in a clockwise direction; currents south of the equator flow in a counterclockwise direction. 2. The large surface currents located within the tropics are warmed by the sun and carry the warm waters away from the equator toward the poles. The farther from the equator and the deeper the waters of the current travel, the colder the water becomes. In their circular journey, current water temperatures change from warm to cold and over again. **Study Question:** Marine life that depends on a current for food may die from lack of food if the current's

direction changes. A directional change in a current may also change water temperature; fish eggs may not hatch as easily or as well as they did before the change.
Page 2a 1. A. Gulf Stream B. California Current C. Humboldt Current D. North Atlantic Current E. Kuroshio Current F. North Equatorial Current G. South Equatorial Current H. West Wind Drift Current I. Brazil Current 2. warm—Kuroshio, South Equatorial, Gulf Stream, Brazil, North Atlantic, and North Equatorial currents; cold—California, Humboldt, West Wind Drift 3. Brazil Current flows counterclockwise, Kuroshio Current flows clockwise 4a. currents b. Gulf Stream, California c. equator, counterclockwise d. West Wind Drift, Antarctica e. climate 5a. Humboldt Current b. currents in the Northern Hemisphere c. North Atlantic Current d. large land masses e. circulating winds 6. Currents provide movement in times of little or no wind.

Page 3 THE OCEAN PROFILE

CONCEPTS: 1. Land formations on the ocean floor are similar to continental land formations. 2. The surface of the ocean floor is continually built up by deposits.

BACKGROUND INFORMATION: Oceans are located in the sunken parts of the earth's surface. These sunken areas are called ocean basins. Continental land masses are areas that rise above the water level of the oceans. The continental shelf, which extends into the ocean about 200 km or more, is really a part of the continent even though it is underwater. Water covering the continental shelf had an average depth of 100 meters. Beyond the continental shelf the edge of the continental land mass drops off sharply and the water deepens abruptly. The steep slope is called the continental slope. The ocean floor, which begins where the continental slope ends, is made up of land formations similar to above-water formations, such as mountains, ridges, rifts, cliffs, valleys, and plains. In the Atlantic Ocean a vast mountain chain, the Mid-Atlantic Ridge, stretches from the vicinity of Greenland to the southern tip of Africa. Some of the mountains in this formation are 3050 meters high. Similar mountain chains exist in the Pacific and Indian oceans. The tops of underwater mountain chains form various islands—Azores, Iceland, Aleutians, Bermuda, and the West Indies. Scientists have discovered that there is a continuous formation of the sea floor at the mid-ocean ridges. Scientists also know that there are large crustal plates which move on the earth's surface. The combination of sea-floor spreading and plate movements causes the formation of underwater mountains, deep trenches, and vast, flat, smooth areas called abyssal plains. The huge trenches may be nearly 11 km in depth. Flat-topped volcanoes, called guyots are found 30 to 60 meters beneath the surface of the water. The entire ocean floor is covered with a deep layer of sediment—mud, sand, and minerals. Rivers continually deposit dissolved minerals into the oceans. The minerals, in addition to the remains of the sea life that sink to the ocean's bottom, gradually build up on the ocean floor.

ENRICHMENT ACTIVITIES: 1. Research how the earth's crust seems to be moving like a conveyor belt from mid-ocean ridges into trenches. 2. Find out how coral reefs are formed.

ANSWER KEY:
Page 3 1. guyots 2. trenches 3. A line with weights was lowered from a ship.
Page 3a. 1. A. shoreline B. continental shelf C. continental slope D. trench E. guyot F. abyssal plain G. ridges H. rift 2a. guyots b. continental slope c. trenches d. abyssal plains e. rifts 3. shoreline 4. approximately 6000 kilometers 5. ridges 6. above water portions of underwater mountains
Page 3b 1. low, tide; sand 2. Sandbar 3. Waves (water), sea cliff 4. Sea stacks 5. Sea cliff, sea arch 6. Rivers emptying into the ocean

Page 4 WAVES

BACKGROUND INFORMATION: Ocean waves are rhythmic patterns made by winds blowing over and against the surface of the water. In the movement of a wave, the water itself is not carried forward, even though it appears to be. Each particle of water tends to move in a circle. The particles are lifted up, carried forward slightly, dropped, and returned to where they started. Waves move forward, but the water does not. Waves have two basic parts, crest and trough. The highest point to which the water rises is called the crest; the lowest point to which the water falls is called the trough. The height of a wave is the distance between trough and crest. Generally speaking, the height of a wave, expressed in meters, will be no more than one half the speed of the wind, expressed in kilometers per hour. Of course, the stronger the wind and the greater the distance over which it blows, the higher the waves will be. The wavelength of a wave is the distance from crest to crest. There are different kinds of waves. The waves that crash ashore with a loud noise are known as surf. Waves of white water, caused by strong winds pushing to water off the tops of waves, are called whitecaps. Waves that break into foam when they hit the shore are called breakers. Breakers occur when the trough of the wave hits the seashore bottom and causes the crest to fall forward. This action causes the wave to break up. Gigantic waves, tsunamis, are mistakenly called tidal waves. The term tidal wave is misleading because tsunamis are not caused by tides but by shock waves from earthquake or volcanic activity at the bottom of the ocean. Tsunamis may be from 18 to 30 meters high; they travel at an average speed of about 724 kilometers per hour. These waves cause extensive damage to life and property when they hit the shore. Endlessly, all over the world, seacoasts are shaped and reshaped by waves' actions. The erosion caused by waves form various coastal features.

ENRICHMENT ACTIVITIES: 1: Research the cause of undertows at certain beaches. Find out about the tsunamis produced by the explosion of Krakatoa in 1883.

ANSWER KEY:
Page 4 1. the tsunami 2. the distance from the bottom of the trough to the top of the crest. **Study Question:** The water molecules move in a circular path, they are lifted up, carried forward, slightly, dropped, and returned.
Page 4a 1. A. crest B. trough C. wavelength D. height 2. The trough hits the seashore bottom, causing the crest to fall 3. Water mixed with air 4. Waves are caused by the friction of surface winds over water 5. tsunami 6. 5 meters/second
Page 4b 1. Tides are greatest during new moon and full moon because the moon's and sun's gravities pull together on earth. 2. Tides are least during first and last quarter moons because the sun and moon pull against each other. 3. because of the rotation of the earth 4. neap 5. 2:50 p.m.

CONCEPTS: 1. Ocean water is made up of approximately 96% pure water and 4% dissolved elements. 2. The two most abundant elements in ocean water are sodium and chlorine, which form sodium chloride, or common salt.

BACKGROUND INFORMATION: Anyone swimming in ocean water has firsthand knowledge of its salt content. It tastes salty, and a crystalline residue forms on one's skin and swimsuit if the ocean water is not rinsed off. The total average mineral content of the major constituents in ocean water is approximately 3.5%. Oceanographers use the term **salinity** to describe the amount of dissolved salts in ocean water. The salinity of ocean water varies from 33 to 37 parts per 1000 (average salinity = 35 parts per 1000). The percentage varies, being somewhat higher in certain subtropical seas and lower where freshwater rivers, such as the Amazon, Mississippi, and Congo, flow into the ocean. Salinity in deeper ocean waters does not vary as much as surface ocean waters. The surface waters are greatly affected by evaporation, precipitation, and run-off from the land. Common salt (sodium chloride) comprises the greatest percentage of the mineral matter of ocean waters. Other salts found with some abundance are magnesium chloride, magnesium sulfate, potassium sulfate, and calcium sulfate. The salinity of ocean waters is caused by rivers washing mineral material from the land into the seas and by volcanic activity both in the oceans and on land. About one-tenth of one percent of ocean water's minerals are traces of various elements and compounds. Discoveries of various metals in solution in the ocean were made many years ago. However, the technology to extract the minerals developed more slowly. Salt can be obtained from ocean water through various processes. One method is to evaporate the water.

ENRICHMENT ACTIVITIES: 1. Find out about the "mining" of minerals from the sea. 2. Find out about icebergs and how they can affect the salinity of ocean waters.

ANSWER KEY:
Page 5 1. Oxygen and hydrogen are the most abundant elements in ocean water. Other elements are sodium and chlorine, which combine to form salt, and other trace elements. 2. The elements iron and aluminum in ocean water are in a dissolved state; to

extract these minute quantities would be very costly.
Study Question: Archimedes' Principle briefly stated is "the buoyant force (upward) is equal to the weight (downward) of fluid pushed aside. The ship floats because it is buoyed up by a force equal to the weight of the liquid displaced by the ship.
Page 5a 1. A. 96.5% B. 1.9% C. 1.1% D. 0.5%
2. E. 3.60% F. 4.73% G. 10.89% H. 77.75%
3a. oxygen, hydrogen b. sodium chloride, salt c. 35, 1000 d. potassium sulfate, calcium sulfate, magnesium sulfate 4a. evaporation and rain b. salinity c. tropical ocean water d. bromine e. calcium carbonate 5. These large rivers pour vast amounts of fresh water into the ocean, thereby reducing the salinity of the nearby ocean waters.
Page 5b 1a. surface b. thermocline c. deep-sea
2. The deeper one goes the lower and colder the temperature becomes; there is a lack of sunlight.
3. 27.81 kg 4a. thermocline b. deep-sea 5. (Accept close answers due to varying estimates of chart values.) a. 195.15 meters, 23°C b. 5486 meters, 563.8 kg c. 161 kg, 3°C 6. 427.45 kg, 3.0°C 7. Manufacturers use very strong, thick materials; the inside pressure is equalized to match the outside pressure.

Page 6 MARINE PLANT LIFE

CONCEPTS: 1. The major plant constituents of ocean water are phytoplankton. 2. Algae and seaweeds are biologically and economically important.

BACKGROUND INFORMATION: In most places the ocean waters teem with life; however, much of it is microscopic in size. These microscopic organisms, both plant and animal, are called plankton. They float through the water at the mercy of waves and currents. The phytoplankton, minute plants, are a variety of species of algae and bacteria. These small plant organisms are a major food supply for animal species, including animal plankton, small fish, penguins, seals, and whales. Certain species of algae, known as seaweeds, are much larger than the phytoplankton. Seaweeds all possess chlorophyll, although the green color might be masked by other pigments. The seaweeds are valuable food sources for a number of marine animals as well as for people. Seaweeds are also an important source of oxygen. Sea lettuce, a common shallow-water seaweed found along the Atlantic and Pacific coasts, looks like lettuce and can be prepared as food for people. The fan kelp is a brown algae with many long, leaflike segments growing from the end of a stalk. A tough, fibrous holdfast anchors the fan kelp to the substratum. This species, rich in iodine and other minerals, is a popular food item in Japan. Most impressive are the giant kelps of the Pacific Ocean coast. The giant kelp grows in shallow water and may reach a length of 450 meters. Its slender stem bears olive-colored leaves which may grow to more than one meter in length. Small air bladders at the base of some leaves give the plant buoyancy. The giant kelp is commercially harvested. The Atlantic coast chenille weed is a beautiful red algae. It grows in quiet waters and is characterized by the delicate hairs on its stem. The chenille does not have an apparent economic importance.

ENRICHMENT ACTIVITIES: 1. Find out about the economic importance of the seaweed called laver and the use of agar, made from certain seaweeds. 2. Find out how the Red Sea receives its color.

ANSWER KEY:
Page 6 1. Phytoplankton are microscopic plants that are the most plentiful and most important food supply to marine life. Giant kelp, a shallow-water plant, may grow to 450 meters tall. It has brown leaves and is harvested commercially. Fan kelp, another brown algae, is rich in iodine and is a popular Japanese food. Sea lettuce, common along the coasts of the Atlantic and Pacific oceans, is a green algae eaten by humans. Red algae is a beautifully colored marine plant.
2. Marine plant life, especially phytoplankton, serves as a good food source for marine animal life; without this food supply, animal life would be in a perilous state of existence. **Study Question:** Algin, a substance made from algae, is used as a smoothing agent and thickener. It keeps ice cream from becoming watery and is used in salad dressings, candy bars, and in the production of synthetic fibers and plastics.
Page 6a 1. A. phytoplankton B. giant kelp C. red algae D. fan kelp E. sea lettuce 2. Circle diatoms. 3a. floating, seaweeds b. sea lettuce, algae c. chlorophyll d. giant kelp, 450 meters 4a. sunlight and minerals b. phytoplankton c. diatoms d. fan kelp e. dinoflagellates 5. There is more sunlight and a good supply of minerals necessary for growth.
Page 6b 1. In the Shore zone during low tide some marine life is out of the water and often burrows into the sand. 2. The Hadal zone is coldest because no sunlight penetrates to its depths. 3. Neritic 4. lack of sunlight 5. Neritic 6. continental shelf 7. plankton, nekton, benthos 8a. neritic b. bathyal/abyssal c. bathyal/abyssal d. shore e. bathyal/abyssal f. bathyal g. abyssal/hadal h. neritic i. neritic 9. plankton 10. (any three) sunlight, temperature, water pressure, salinity, food supply

Page 7 MARINE ANIMAL LIFE: Shallow Water

CONCEPTS: 1. The shallow and uppermost regions of ocean water support a diverse community of animal life. 2. The seashore community is subjected to a wide range of environmental changes.

BACKGROUND INFORMATION: The ocean is a vast storehouse of animal life. The surface waters teem with tiny animals called zooplankton. These microscopic creatures include foraminifers, radiolarians, copepods, and the larvae of shrimp, snails, worms, and various fish. Rich supplies of plankton organisms serve as food for a great variety of sea creatures. Various fish feed on plankton and are, in turn, preyed upon by larger animals, such as the barracuda and sea turtle. The sea anemone, a coelenterate, also eats fish. The anemone's fingerlike tentacles paralyze fish with tiny poison threads and pull the prey to the anemone's mouth. The jellyfish, another coelenterate, is also noted for its stinging tentacles. The large Portuguese man-of-war is a danger to swimmers. Starfish belong to the phylum of spiny-skinned animals, the Echinoderms. They have five to ten arms, each with many small, tubelike feet that move them over the ocean bottom in search of food—clams and oysters. The sea is the greatest habitat for the crustaceans, which include crabs, lobsters, and shrimp. Every seacoast vacationer soon becomes a shell collector. Shells are the home of a very abundant class of mostly aquatic animals, the mollusks. This group includes not only the bivalves such as scallops and oysters, the univalves such as snails, but also the octopus and squid. Some organisms are fixed to one spot in their adult life. These creatures, such as the barnacles and sponges, are referred to as benthos organisms. Those that are free-swimming are termed nekton organisms. Examples of nekton are fish and turtles. The animals living near the seashore are subjected to a wide range of changes in their environment—changes in surface temperature of water, in tides affecting currents, and in salinity, which fluctuates when the ocean is diluted by freshwater streams.

ENRICHMENT ACTIVITIES: 1. Research the lives of the horseshoe crab, hermit crab, and comb jelly. 2. Research the defensive activities of the puffers, flying fish, and flounders.

ANSWER KEY:
Page 7 1. Answers may vary. For example: zooplankton, small fish, barracuda 2. horseshoe crab

Study Question: *echinoderms:* starfish; *crustaceans:* crab, lobster; *mollusks:* scallops, octopus; *fish:* barracuda, flying fish; *reptiles:* turtle

Page 7a 1. A. sea turtle B. zooplankton C. flying fish D. jellyfish E. barracuda F. crab G. horseshoe crab H. starfish I. octopus J. lobster K. scallops L. coral M. sea anemone 2. lobster 3. scallop 4. octopus 5. flying fish 6. Coral 7. It poisons prey and pulls it to its mouth with tentacles. 8. barracuda

Page 8   MARINE ANIMAL LIFE: Deep Water

CONCEPT: The ocean depths, a stable environment, have a very specialized community of life.

BACKGROUND INFORMATION: Sunlight penetrates to a depth of about 30 meters in clear ocean water, but some sunrays may reach 450 meters. The temperature in deep ocean water is generally –1°C. The greater activity of life is therefore in the uppermost regions of ocean water. Several fish species venture to depths of about 150 meters. The codfish, tuna, and shark are examples. In the twilight zone, the region of very weak light, the curious-looking hatchet fish can be found. This is also the haunt of the giant squid. This mollusk, which can reach a length of 15 meters, is the basic food of the large sperm whale. For many years scientists did not believe that life could exist below 450 meters. However, deep-sea explorations since the late 1800s have provided specimens from great depths. Studying deep-water specimens is often difficult since some fish puff up when they are brought to the surface due to the tremendous change in pressure. Many deep-sea fish have bizarre appendages and phosphorescent organs that adapt them to their pitch-black environment. These luminescent organs attract other fish as prey and help the species recognize its own kind. The viperfish has a formidable mouth with large, fanglike teeth. Its sides are lined with rows of luminous dots. The shrimplike prawn, a bright red crustacean, is a staple food of many deep-sea fish. The tiny chiasmodon fish is capable of extending its stomach in order to feed on prey much larger than itself. Deep-water explorations have revealed the presence of sea spiders, sea urchins, and brittle stars at depths lower than 1800 meters. In some places where geothermal vents release heated water rich in minerals, unique communities exist. Bacteria utilize the minerals to synthesize organic compounds. In turn some of the bacteria have symbiotic relationships with mollusks and giant tube worms.

ENRICHMENT ACTIVITIES: 1. Research the chemosynthetic process which takes place at geothermal vent communities ("black smokers"). 2. Find out about the bioluminescence of deep-sea fish.

ANSWER KEY:
Page 8 1. giant squid 2. The absence of light does not allow plant growth. **Study Question:** various minerals, such as hydrogen sulfide
Page 8a 1. A. prawn B. giant squid C. hatchet fish D. viperfish E. chiasmodon F. brittle stars G. giant tube worm 2. giant squid 3. chiasmodon 4. Prawns 5. to attract prey or for species recognition 6. Their great internal pressure causes them to swell up when they are at sea level pressure.

Page 9   SUBMERSIBLES: DEEP-DIVING VEHICLES

CONCEPT: Submersibles are deep-diving vehicles used for underwater exploration.

BACKGROUND INFORMATION: Ocean exploration is as exciting as space exploration. Adventures into this unknown have intrigued people since the earliest times. In the early 1930s, two Americans, William Beebe and Otis Barton, descended 930 meters into the ocean depths in an iron sphere (bathysphere) suspended by a cable. In 1960 a Swiss scientist, August Piccard, descended to 10,910 meters in a vessel, the *Trieste,* he designed for the U.S. Navy. These kinds of deep-ocean exploration vessels were known as bathyscaphes. They consist of a float and a spherical gondola for the passengers. The float is filled with gasoline, which is lighter than water and provides lifting power. To descend, the air in the vessel's tanks is expelled and seawater is taken in. This causes the vessel to become more dense than water and it sinks. When the vessel reaches the desired depth, its buoyancy is controlled by the release of iron pellets. The release of the iron ballast is controlled by the command-operator in quantities that will achieve the desired speed of ascent. Some horizontal movement is possible through the use of propellers powered by battery-driven electric motors. The gondola is the observation/instrument cabin. It is usually very small, about two meters in diameter inside. Mercury-vapor searchlights are used to illuminate the ocean around the vessel. To withstand the tremendous pressure under the sea, the walls of the gondola are 12 cm in thickness. Since the *Trieste,* a variety of vessels known as submersibles have been built to explore the ocean depths. The *Deepstar* vessel carried a crew of three; the *Aluminaut* carried six. The *Alvin,* which was used to explore the remains of the *Titanic,* had a crew of three and very sophisticated electronic equipment.

ENRICHMENT ACTIVITIES: 1. Research the various biological and geological discoveries made by submersibles. 2. Find out how carbon dioxide is removed from the atmosphere in the cabin.

ANSWER KEY:
Page 9 1. batteries 2. Pilots use manipulator arms to pick up objects outside the vessel. **Study Question:** A small, robot vessel connected to *Alvin* by cables and controlled by the pilot, was sent into the *Titanic* and took video pictures of its surroundings.
Page 9a 1. A. gondola B. hatch C. manipulator arm D. motor E. flotation tanks F. battery storage G. iron ballast H. sonar unit 2. Air is released so that seawater enters the tanks and makes the vessel heavier than water. 3. The operator releases the iron ballast. 4. sonar units 5. through the hatch 6. The walls are made of thick metal and the inside of the vessel is pressurized.

Page 10 SNORKELING AND SCUBA DIVING

CONCEPT: Underwater exploration has been greatly facilitated by the use of the snorkel and the invention of the aqualung.

BACKGROUND INFORMATION: Since early times people have desired to explore beneath the sea. The first attempts were simply dives below the water's surface with the divers holding their breaths. Subsequent attempts included holding an overturned vessel over one's head and using the trapped air as an oxygen supply. This was, of course, also limiting. The use of hollow reeds to breathe the air above the water surface offered unlimited air but restricted attainable depths. Snorkeling, a popular means of exploring the ocean, is much like this latter method. The snorkel is a J-shaped breathing tube with a mouthpiece. It eliminates the need to raise one's head above water for air. A snorkel makes below-surface exploration easy because a person can breathe while keeping his or her face in the water. It is also possible to dive with the open snorkel tube in one's mouth. The pressure of the air from holding one's breath keeps water from entering the lungs. The average length of a snorkel dive is about 25-30 seconds; the average depth of a snorkel dive is about 8-10 meters.

In 1943 the French naval captain, Jacques-Yves Cousteau, and his associate, Emile Gagnan, an engineer, invented the aqualung. With this invention, extended free-diving came into existence. The aqualung consists of tanks of compressed gas with a regulator to supply the diver with needed oxygen via a connecting hose. A mouthpiece is held between the teeth. A weighted belt helps maintain buoyancy. Rubber fins or flippers fit over the feet and increase the pushing and maneuvering abilities of the legs and feet. The face mask allows the diver to see better. A depth gauge, an important instrument strapped to the diver's wrist, lets the diver know his or her exact depth. A diver risks serious internal injuries if he or she surfaces too rapidly from great depths. The diver may wear a wet suit made of a rubberlike material. The suit helps to retain body heat and protects the diver against exposure. A number of instruments and gadgets have been developed to aid the free-swimming diver in underwater work. A spear gun that operates on compressed air or carbon dioxide is used for spear fishing and for protection. Underwater cameras have been perfected for still photographs, motion pictures, and television broadcasts from the ocean depths. Small, electrically-powered submarines carry a diver around and allow him or her to extend the range of exploration. Diving that uses "self-contained underwater breathing apparatus" is called *scuba* diving. Not only is it a popular sport, but it is a useful method for biological and geological underwater exploration.

ENRICHMENT ACTIVITIES: 1. Find out about outdated diving suits and diving bells. 2. Find out about the hazards of scuba diving called the "bends" and "rapture of the deep."

ANSWER KEY:
Page 10 1. Snorkelers and scuba divers both use flippers or fins, a face mask, and some type of breathing device—either a snorkel or an aqualung. Both may use an underwater camera or a spear gun. 2. A scuba diver uses an aqualung, a self-contained supply of air. **Study Question:** The aqualung, an important breakthrough in deep-sea exploration, freed the diver from air lines or heavy weights. The air supply is strapped to the diver's back in cylinders. These high-pressure cylinders with regulators automatically adjust breathing air to the same pressure as the surrounding water. The aqualung provides the scuba diver with air at exactly the right pressure.
Page 10a 1. A. snorkel B. flippers/fins C. regulator D. face mask E. face mask F. camera G. air tank (aqualung) H. air hose I. weight belt J. depth guage

K. spear gun L. wet suit M. fins/flippers 2. Circle fins/flippers and face mask. 3a. weight belt b. fins, quickly c. wet suits d. waterproof e. face mask 4a. scuba b. spear gun c. the bends d. regulator e. snorkel 5. lack of air supply, water pressure, hostile marine life, temperature changes

Page 11 TOOLS OF OCEANOGRAPHY

CONCEPT: Oceanographers use various tools to study the chemical and physical properties of the ocean.

BACKGROUND INFORMATION: Early oceanographers had to use inefficient methods to explore the ocean's secrets. However, as scientific exploration of the ocean progressed, instruments to aid in the exploration were developed; the tools of oceanographers became increasingly efficient. Early oceanographers relied on chance discoveries of deep-sea objects pulled aboard ship by dredge nets and grappling hooks. Microscopic plankton life, therefore, was not efficiently collected until extremely fine mesh nets were used. Early oceanographers determined ocean depths by using measured ropes or cables. These tools were inaccurate and difficult to use. With the advent of radar and sonar instruments, an electronic depth recorder was developed. This instrument operates on the echo-sounding principle. A device sends sound waves from the ship's bottom to the ocean bottom. These sound waves are reflected back from the ocean floor to the ship much like an echo. A timer records and calculates the time for the transmission and return of the sound wave. Using this information, a computer determines the depth. A recorder may be used to produce a graph of the depths of the ocean bottom. Oceanographers can measure the speed of ocean currents with an instrument called a current meter. The meter's propeller, when placed in an ocean current, spins from the current's force. The current meter records the number of revolutions of the propeller per unit of time. From this measurement, the current speed is calculated. The current meter can also indicate the average current direction. Samples of the ocean bottom substratum can be collected with a corer. The corer is attached to a steel cable and lowered to the ocean floor. A heavy weight on top drives the hollow tube into the sediment. When the corer returns to the ship, sediments within the tube are removed for study. Water samples from various depths can be collected by the Nansen collector. This instrument is constructed so that it can trap a sample of water at a specific level below the surface.

ENRICHMENT ACTIVITIES: 1. Find out about other tools of oceanography such as: swallow floats, trawl nets, and hydrographic casts. 2. Find out about the various specialized fields of oceanography: physical oceanography, chemical oceanography, biological oceanography, and marine geology.

ANSWER KEY:
Page 11 1. A **current meter** is used to determine speed and direction of currents. A **depth recorder** uses the echo-sounding principle by sending a sound wave to the ocean bottom and recording the length of time the echo takes to reach the ship. A **corer** collects samples of substratum on and beneath the ocean floor. A **plankton collecting net** is a very fine mesh net that collects microscopic plant and animal life in the ocean water. A **Nansen bottle** traps water samples at specific levels or depths. 2. Studies by oceanographers indicate vast deposits of oil and natural gas below the bottom of the ocean. Many of these deposits are located in offshore land areas, and some nations are already drilling and tapping these deposits. In the future these deposits may become vital when present day supplies become depleted.
Study Question: A floating instrument platform called *FLIP* resembles an ordinary ship. However, when the tanks in its long hull are filled with water, the stern (rear) of the ship sinks. Its bow (front) rises vertically and becomes a stationary oceanographic research laboratory.
Page 11a 1. A. plankton collecting net B. depth recorder C. current meter D. corer E. Nansen bottle water sampler 2. Circle plankton collecting net.
3a. corer b. Nansen bottle c. current meter d. depth recorder 4a. water sampler b. corer c. depth recorder d. collecting net e. current meter 5. Much equipment used in the field of oceanography is relatively new and recently developed; many scientists consider oceanography as the "last frontier."

Page 12 THE OCEAN'S STOREHOUSE

CONCEPTS: 1. Throughout history the oceans have provided a variety of materials for people. 2. Modern technology has aided in discovering new products from the ocean and the means of extracting them.

BACKGROUND INFORMATION: Early peoples living on the shores of marine water discovered plants, animals, and minerals that they could use. In our modern world we are still using the resources of the ocean's storehouse. The oceans enable ships to transport food, supplies, minerals, oil, and people from one part of the globe to another. Well-established fishing grounds supply millions of people with a relatively inexpensive food item. Whales are still hunted for their oil and blubber. Seals and sea otters are hunted for their hides. These practices have caused certain animals to become endangered. Various minerals such as salt, magnesium, gypsum, borax, and potassium are extracted from seawater. Underwater petroleum deposits are located and tapped. Pearls and coral are valuable resources for jewelry. The ocean's role in the global water cycle is tremendous. Evaporation from the oceans produces the water vapor which condenses over our land masses and provides the fresh water we need for drinking, preparing foods, washing, manufacturing, and growing crops. In some areas desalinization, changing salt water into fresh water, is necessary to provide local freshwater needs. As we use the ocean's storehouse, we must recognize the need for conservation and make serious efforts not to pollute the ocean.

ENRICHMENT ACTIVITIES: 1. Research the present status of these ocean industries: whaling, sponge gathering, and seal hunting. 2. Find out how cultured pearls are made.

ANSWER KEY:
Page 12 1. The ocean is the greatest source of evaporation to produce fresh water. 2. A variety of cargoes are shipped via the ocean, such as oil, minerals, lumber, automobiles, meat, fruit, steel, coal, and so on. **Study Question:** Manganese nodules are most numerous in the South Pacific Ocean and can be gathered with dredges or trawls.
Page 12a 1. 1. fish, seaweed 2. Pearls, coral 3. petroleum and natural gas 4. sponges 5. Oil spilled from tankers has polluted the water, killed marine life, and spoiled beaches. 6. The salt and other minerals must be removed.

A LAST LOOK—PART I

A. 1. Indian Ocean does not belong. It is an ocean; the North Sea and the Gulf of Mexico are seas.
2. Continental shelf does not belong. Crest and trough are parts of a wave. Continental shelf is part of the ocean floor.
3. Neon does not belong. It is not a common ocean water element. Sodium and chlorine are.
4. Fish does not belong. Kelp and algae are ocean plants. Fish is an animal.
5. Stethoscope does not belong. A corer and depth recorder are oceanographic tools. A stethoscope is a medical tool.
6. Oar does not belong. Wet suit and air tank are pieces of underwater diving equipment.
7. California Current does not belong. It is a cold current whereas the Gulf Stream and Kuroshio Current are warm.
8. Flying fish does not belong. They live near the ocean's surface; prawns and viperfish live in deeper parts.
9. Coal does not belong. It is a land resource; oil and magnesium are ocean resources.
10. Snorkel does not belong. *Alvin* and a bathyscaphe are submersibles. A snorkel is used for diving near the surface.

Note: These are suggested answers, each determined by a specific viewpoint. Since more than one correct answer is possible, accept any reasonable answer student can justify.

B. 1. salt
2. moon, sun, tides
3. California, Gulf Stream
4. self-contained underwater breathing apparatus
5. plankton
6. wind, water
7. Pacific, Atlantic, Indian, seas
8. sunlight, cold/low
9. clockwise
10. shallow, deep

Note: If the ability of the students might prohibit them from writing the words required to complete Part B of this page, the answers might be randomly displayed on the chalkboard or bulletin board.

A LAST LOOK—PART II

A bathyscaphe or *Nereid*
B. a submersible

A. giant kelp
B. shallow water plant

A. Mediterranean Sea
B. a sea

A. guyot
B. flat-top volcano

A. wave
B. a tsunami

A. giant squid
B. deep-ocean-zone life

A. North Equatorial Current
B. above equator

A. diatoms
B. abundant plant life

A. trench
B. marine trench

A. snorkel
B. shallow-water apparatus

A. current meter
B. measures speed

A. sponge
B. attached plantlike creature

A LAST LOOK—PART III

A. 1. l
   2. a
   3. e
   4. j
   5. f
   6. k
   7. d
   8. i
   9. b
  10. g

B. 1. gondola
   2. trenches
   3. Tsunamis
   4. desalinization
   5. continental shelf
   6. 3.5
   7. Pacific
   8. scallop
   9. air tank
  10. phytoplankton

A LAST LOOK—PART IV

A. The ocean is teeming with life even though the people fishing don't catch anything.

B. 1. Arrow points to continental shelf, not the slope.
   2. The picture shows a corer, used to obtain core samples.
   3. Person is scuba diving, not snorkeling.
   4. Wavelength is distance from one crest to the adjacent crest. Picture shows two wavelengths.

C.

Across	**Down**
1. Shrimp	1. scuba
2. shell	2. sea
3. submersible	
4. algae	
5. Atlantic	

Oceans and Seas of the World

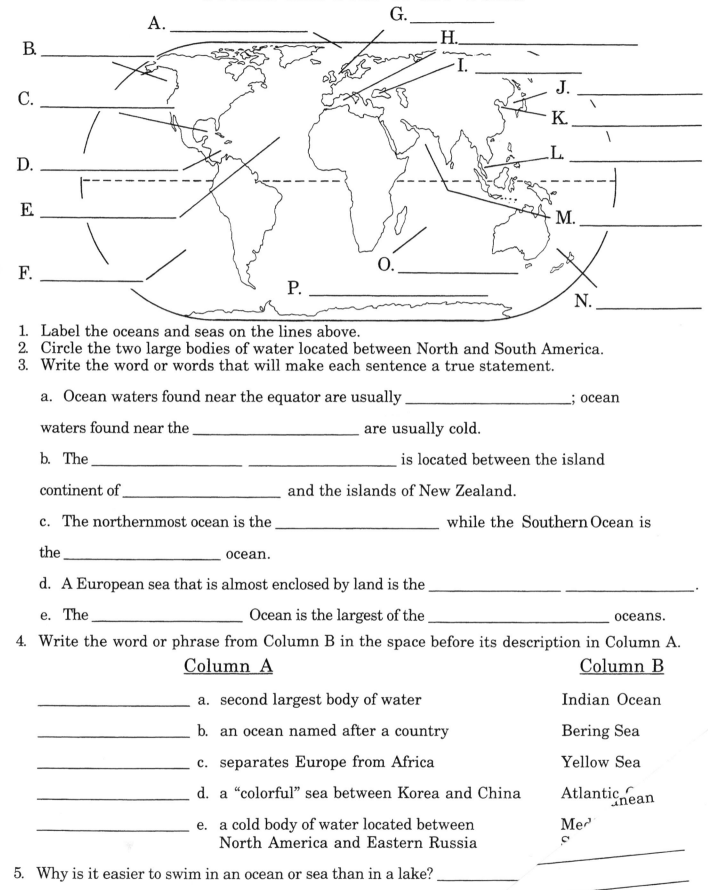

A. _____
B. _____
C. _____
D. _____
E. _____
F. _____
G. _____
H. _____
I. _____
J. _____
K. _____
L. _____
M. _____
N. _____
O. _____
P. _____

1. Label the oceans and seas on the lines above.
2. Circle the two large bodies of water located between North and South America.
3. Write the word or words that will make each sentence a true statement.

   a. Ocean waters found near the equator are usually _____; ocean

   waters found near the _____ are usually cold.

   b. The _____ _____ is located between the island

   continent of _____ and the islands of New Zealand.

   c. The northernmost ocean is the _____ while the Southern Ocean is

   the _____ ocean.

   d. A European sea that is almost enclosed by land is the _____ _____.

   e. The _____ Ocean is the largest of the _____ oceans.

4. Write the word or phrase from Column B in the space before its description in Column A.

   ### Column A

   _____ a. second largest body of water

   _____ b. an ocean named after a country

   _____ c. separates Europe from Africa

   _____ d. a "colorful" sea between Korea and China

   _____ e. a cold body of water located between
   North America and Eastern Russia

   ### Column B

   Indian Ocean

   Bering Sea

   Yellow Sea

   Atlantic Ocean

   Med
   S

5. Why is it easier to swim in an ocean or sea than in a lake? _____

   _____

Oceanography

© Milliken Publishing Company

1a

Major Ocean Currents

A. _____

B. _____
_____

C. _____

D. _____

E. _____

F. _____

G. _____
_____

H. _____

I. _____

1. Label the ocean currents on the lines above.
2. Circle six warm ocean currents and put a check mark above three cold ocean currents.
3. Draw arrows showing directional flow of the Brazil and Kuroshio currents.
4. Write the word or words that will make each sentence a true statement.

   a. The phrase "rivers within an ocean" refers to the ocean's _____ .

   b. Two ocean currents that affect the coasts of North America are the _____

   and _____ currents.

   c. The currents below the _____ flow in a _____ direction.

   d. The _____ current, in the Southern Hemisphere, completely circles the

   cold continent of _____.

   e. Currents affect the _____ of neighboring regions.

5. Write the word or phrase from Column B in the space before its description in Column A.

Column A	Column B
_____ a. a cold South American coastal current	North Atlantic Current
_____ b. eastward flowing "rivers"	Humboldt Current
_____ c. a warm ocean current affecting England's climate	currents in the Northern Hemisphere
_____ d. cause currents to change directions	large land masses
_____ e. push surface water in different directions	circulating winds

6. Why did ocean-going boats depend on ocean currents? _____

_____

© Milliken Publishing Company

Oceanography

The Ocean Profile

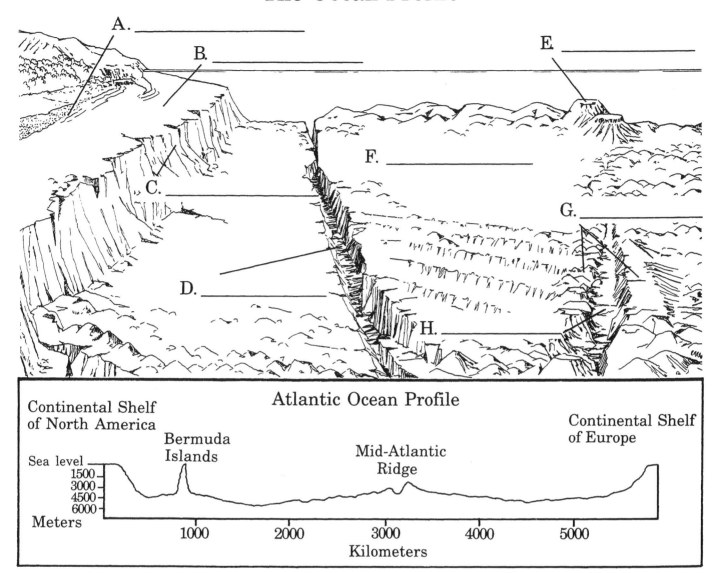

A. _____

B. _____

C. _____

D. _____

E. _____

F. _____

G. _____

H. _____

Atlantic Ocean Profile

Continental Shelf
of North America

Bermuda
Islands

Mid-Atlantic
Ridge

Continental Shelf
of Europe

Sea level

1500
3000
4500
6000

Meters

1000   2000   3000   4000   5000

Kilometers

1. Label the ocean profile features on the lines above.
2. Identify these features of the ocean basin:

   a. underwater volcanic mountains _____

   b. land from continent's edge to ocean floor _____

   c. narrow, very deep valleys _____

   d. flat, nearly level areas _____

   e. valleys between ridges _____

3. The line which marks the edge of ocean water on land is called the _____

4. What is the distance of the ocean profile shown in the chart above? _____

5. Of what features do great underwater mountain ranges consist? ___

6. What are islands? _____

Oceanography

© Milliken Publishing Company

3a

Features of the Coastline

sea cliff

river valley

bay

beach

sea stacks

sea arch

sandbar

beaches are the areas between the _____ tide and high _____

y beaches are made of millions of tiny quartz particles called _____.

4. Tall, n___ried by waves may form a _____ across the mouth of a river bay.

5. Waves may cu___ n action of _____ may form a high wall of rock called

___ along an ocean coast.

6. What is an important __cks along seacoasts are known as _____.

_____ and form a tunnel, called a _____.

diments deposited in the sea? _____

© Milliken Publishing Company

Waves

A. _____

B. _____

C. _____

D. _____

Whitecaps Strong wind pushes water off top of wave.

Breakers Trough hits bottom, crest falls, wave breaks up.

Tsunamis

average speed: 750 kilometers/hour   height: 15-30 meters

1. Label the parts of a wave on the lines above.

2. Breakers form when _____

3. What is the white of whitecap waves? _____

4. What causes ocean waves? _____

5. A special kind of wave is the _____, which can cause severe destruction.

6. The period of a wave is the length of time for one wavelength to pass a given point.

   Speed of a wave = $\dfrac{\text{wavelength}}{\text{period}}$

   What is the speed of a wave that has a wavelength of 20m and a period of four seconds?

   _____

Tides

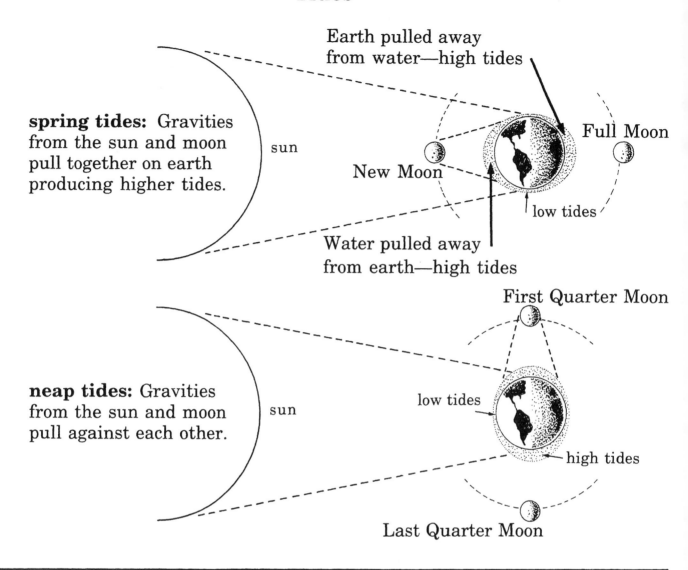

spring tides: Gravities from the sun and moon pull together on earth producing higher tides.

Earth pulled away from water—high tides

Full Moon

New Moon

sun

low tides

Water pulled away from earth—high tides

First Quarter Moon

neap tides: Gravities from the sun and moon pull against each other.

sun

low tides

high tides

Last Quarter Moon

Rotation of the earth causes two low and two high tides each day. Tomorrow's tides are about fifty minutes later than today's tides.

1. During what phases of the moon are the tides the highest? Why? _____

   _____

2. During what phases of the moon are the tides the lowest? Why? _____

   _____

3. Why are there two high tides and two low tides each day? _____

4. The lowest high tides are called _____ tides.

5. If the first high tide of today is at 2:00 p.m., what will be the approximate time of

   tomorrow's first high tide? _____

Characteristics of Ocean Water

Major Elements in Ocean Water (Element)................. (%)

oxygen ....
hydrogen................... } A. _____
chlorine.................... B. _____
sodium .... C. _____
magnesium...........
sulfur.......................
calcium...................
potassium...............
bromine...................
carbon..................... } D. _____
iron..........................
strontium ....
silicon......................
fluorine ....
aluminum...............
phosphorus...........

Common Salts in Ocean Water

other salt traces (0.1%)
magnesium bromide (0.21%)
calcium carbonate (0.35%)
potassium sulfate (2.46%)
calcium sulfate
E. _____

magnesium sulfate
F. _____

magnesium chloride
G. _____

sodium chloride
H. _____

1. On lines A-D above, write the percentages of elements found in ocean water: 1.1%, 0.5%, 96.5,% and 1.9%.
2. On lines E-H above, write the percentage per 1000 of common salts found in ocean water: 77.75%, 3.60%, 10.89%, and 4.73%.
3. Write the word or words that will make each sentence a true statement.
   a. The two most abundant elements in the form of dissolved gases found in ocean water are

   _____ and _____ .

   b. When sodium and chlorine unite they form _____ _____ ,

   commonly called _____ .

   c. The average salinity of ocean water is _____ parts per _____ .

   d. Three sulfurous salt compounds found in ocean water are _____ ,

   _____ , and _____ .
4. Write the word or phrase from Column B in the space before its description in Column A.

   <u>Column A</u>   <u>Column B</u>

   _____   a. affects surface salinity of ocean water   salinity

   _____   b. amount of dissolved salts in ocean water   bromine

   _____   c. above average salt content   evaporation and rain

   _____   d. element extracted from ocean water   tropical ocean water

   _____   e. used by marine animals in shells   calcium carbonate

5. Why is ocean water salinity greatly reduced at the mouths of the Amazon, Congo, and

   Mississippi rivers? _____

Pressure and Temperature of Ocean Water

Ocean water pressure increases 1.03 kg per square cm (14.7 lbs. per square in.) for every 10 meters (33 feet) of depth.

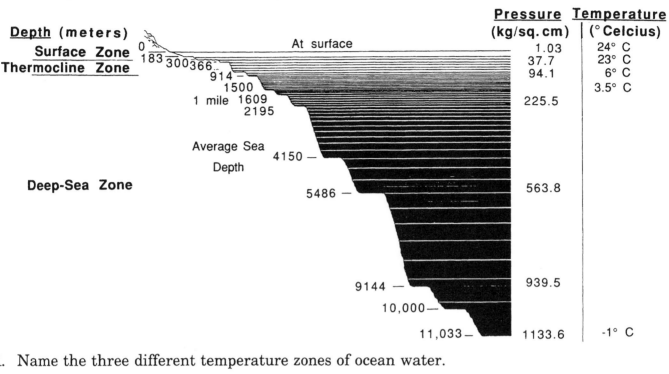

1. Name the three different temperature zones of ocean water.

   a. _____   b. _____   c. _____

2. What happens to ocean temperatures the deeper one goes? Why? _____

   _____

3. How much pressure is on an object having an area of 9 sq. cm at 30 meters deep? _____

4. a. Which zone has the widest range in temperature? _____

   b. Which zone has the coldest temperature? _____

5. Compute the following measurements per sq. cm:

Depth	**Pressure**	**Temperature (approx.)**
a. _____	20.1 kg	_____
b. _____	_____	2° C
c. 1 mile	_____	_____

6. What would be the approximate pressure and temperature at the average ocean depth?

   _____

7. How do makers of deep-sea diving equipment and submersibles compensate for the

   tremendous pressure placed upon their products? _____

   _____

Marine Plant Life

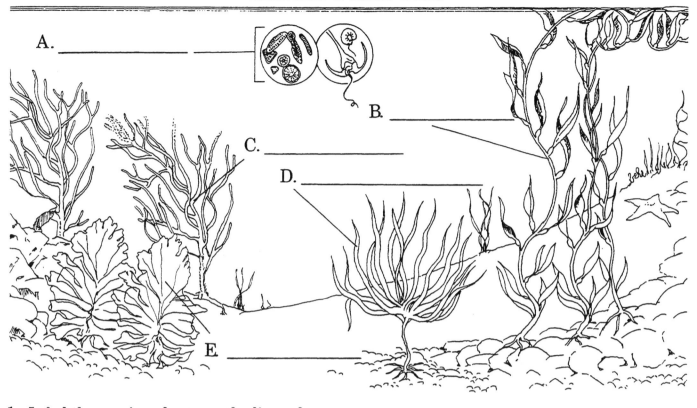

A. _____

B. _____

C. _____

D. _____

E. _____

1. Label the marine plants on the lines above.
2. Circle the picture of the most abundant form of microscopic plant life.
3. Write the word or words that will make each sentence a true statement.

   a. Forms of plankton move about in the water by _____, but _____
   cannot because they are anchored.

   b. The green, leaflike part of the _____ is edible and is a common form of

   shallow-water _____ .

   c. Both land and sea plants have the important green coloring substance called _____ .

   d. The very large sea plant called _____ may grow as tall as _____ .

4. Write the word or phrase from Column B in the space before its description in Column A.

<table>
<tr><th colspan="2">Column A</th><th>Column B</th></tr>
<tr><td>_____</td><td>a. needed by all plant life</td><td>diatoms</td></tr>
<tr><td>_____</td><td>b. plankton plant life</td><td>sunlight and minerals</td></tr>
<tr><td>_____</td><td>c. most abundant form of phytoplankton</td><td>fan kelp</td></tr>
<tr><td>_____</td><td>d. an anchored marine plant</td><td>dinoflagellates</td></tr>
<tr><td>_____</td><td>e. microscopic plankton with "tails"</td><td>phytoplankton</td></tr>
</table>

5. Why do marine plants grow most thickly near ocean shores and coasts? _____

_____

Ocean "Life Zones"

Zones	Shore	Neritic	Bathyal	Abyssal	Hadal
Limits	Between low and high tide lines	Low tide line to end of Continental Shelf	Continenetal Shelf downward	From 2000 meters downward	Long, narrow oceanic trenches
Depth	shallow	about 200 m	about 2000 m	about 6000 m	more than 6000 m
Temperature	about 24° C	about 23° C	less than 10° C	less than 4° C	1.2° to 3.6° C
Sunlight Penetration	yes	yes	very little	no	no
Marine Life	•Plankton •Nekton •Benthos seaweed, mussels, crabs, flounder clams, barnacles	•Plankton •Nekton herring, octopus, porpoises, rays, anchovies, angelfish, kelp	•Nekton •Benthos oyster, sealily, large whales, giant squid, kelp	•Benthos sea cucumbers, brittle stars, odd-looking fish	•Benthos sea urchins, worms with no mouth or stomach

Types of Marine Life

•**Plankton:** microscopic plants and animals that float at or near ocean surface where sunlight is ample: diatoms, copepods, dinoflagellates, jellyfish

•**Nekton:** mostly fish and other animals that can swim fast in search of food or for safety: cod, halibut, whales, seals, turtles, squid, sea horse, eel

•**Benthos:** plants and animals associated with ocean bottom for entire life: seaweed, coral, sponge, starfish, clams, snails, lobster

1. Name the zone where marine life sometimes lives out of water. Why? _____

   _____

2. Which zone has the coldest water? Why? _____

   _____

3. In which zone do commercial fishermen seek large catches? _____

4. Why is seaweed unable to grow beyond the Bathyal zone? _____

5. Which zone, neritic or abyssal, has the greatest variety of marine life? _____

6. What underwater land area is the "dividing line" between the neritic and bathyal zones? _____

   _____

7. Name the major groups of plant and animal life found in the ocean. _____

   _____

8. In which zones will you probably find the following?

   a. tuna _____ b. blue whale _____ c. oysters _____

   d. barnacles _____ e. deep-sea angler _____ f. giant squid _____

   g. "see through" fish _____ h. sharks _____ i. sea lions _____

9. Which important type of life is the main food source for larger marine life? _____

10. Name three factors that affect marine life. _____

Marine Animal Life: Shallow Water

A. _____

B. _____

C. _____

D. _____

E. _____

F. _____

G. _____

H. _____

I. _____

J. _____

K. _____

L. _____

M. _____

1. Label the animals shown on the lines above.

2. Which animal has antennae and five pairs of legs? _____

3. To escape predators the _____ snaps its two shells together and jets away.

4. The _____ is recognized by its eight long tentacles with suction cups.

5. Using its winglike fins, the _____ skims over the surface of the water.

6. _____ are tiny animals which live in colonies that form rocklike, branching structures.

7. How does the sea anemone capture its prey? _____

8. The _____ is often known as the "tiger" of the sea.

Marine Animal Life: Deep Water

A. _____

B. _____

C. _____

D. _____

E. _____

F. _____

G. _____

1. Label the deep-sea animals on the lines above.
2. What deep-sea animal has often been called a "sea monster"? _____

3. Which fish is able to eat prey many times larger than itself ? _____

4. _____ are also known as shrimp.

5. For what possible purpose are the luminescent organs seen on fish B and E above? _____

    _____

6. Why do some fish puff up when they are brought to the surface from ocean depths? _____

    _____

Submersibles: Deep-Diving Vehicles

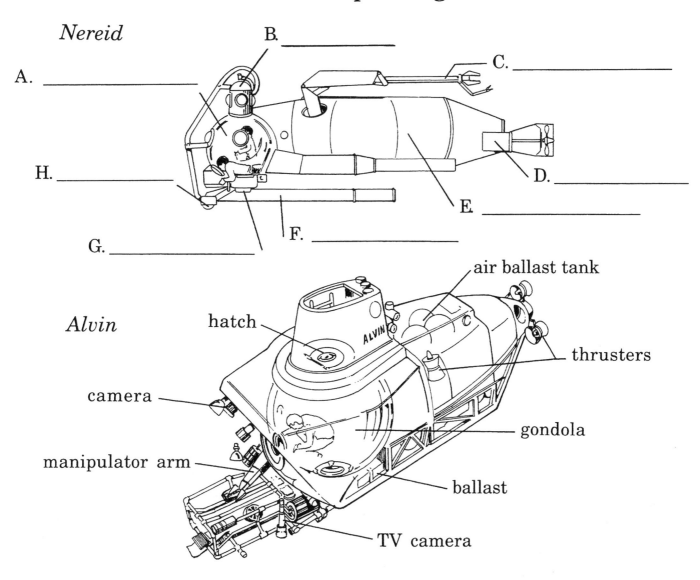

Nereid

A. _____

B. _____

C. _____

H. _____

D. _____

E. _____

G. _____

F. _____

Alvin

air ballast tank

hatch

thrusters

camera

gondola

manipulator arm

ballast

TV camera

1. Label the parts of the submersible, the *Nereid,* on the lines above.

2. How is a submersible made heavier to allow it to descend? _____

_____

3. How is the submersible made lighter to allow it to ascend? _____

_____

4. What instrument in submersibles allows pilots to determine their location and depth?

_____

5. How do the pilot and scientist get into the gondola? _____

6. Why doesn't the great pressure of the deep water crush the walls of the submersible?

_____

_____

Snorkeling and Scuba Diving

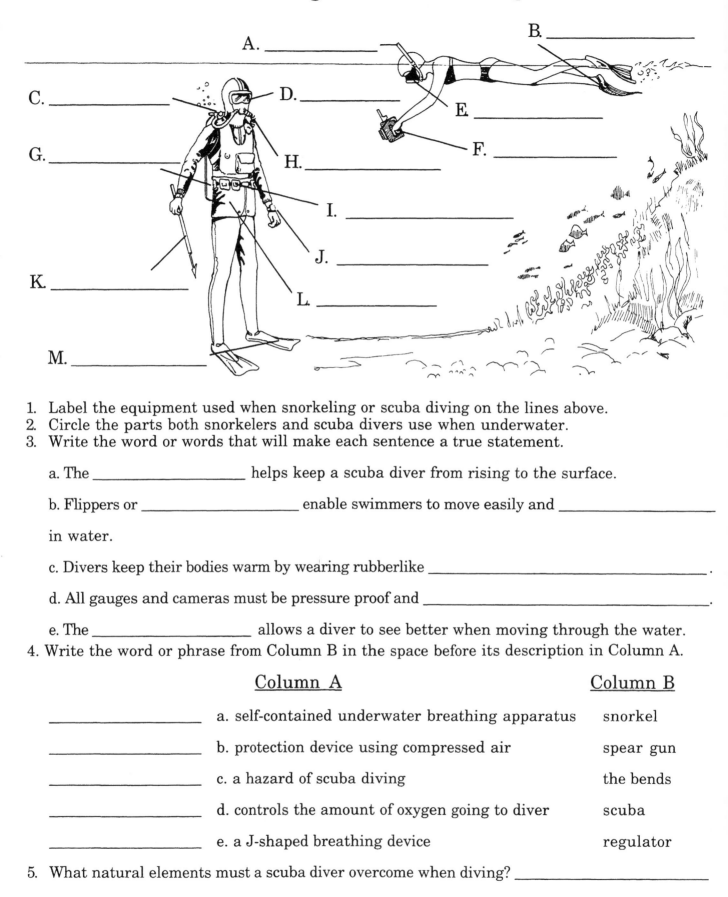

A. _____

B. _____

C. _____

D. _____

E. _____

F. _____

G. _____

H. _____

I. _____

J. _____

K. _____

L. _____

M. _____

1. Label the equipment used when snorkeling or scuba diving on the lines above.
2. Circle the parts both snorkelers and scuba divers use when underwater.
3. Write the word or words that will make each sentence a true statement.

   a. The _____ helps keep a scuba diver from rising to the surface.

   b. Flippers or _____ enable swimmers to move easily and _____

   in water.

   c. Divers keep their bodies warm by wearing rubberlike _____.

   d. All gauges and cameras must be pressure proof and _____.

   e. The _____ allows a diver to see better when moving through the water.
4. Write the word or phrase from Column B in the space before its description in Column A.

<u>Column A</u>   <u>Column B</u>

_____ a. self-contained underwater breathing apparatus   snorkel

_____ b. protection device using compressed air   spear gun

_____ c. a hazard of scuba diving   the bends

_____ d. controls the amount of oxygen going to diver   scuba

_____ e. a J-shaped breathing device   regulator

5. What natural elements must a scuba diver overcome when diving? _____

_____

Tools of Oceanography

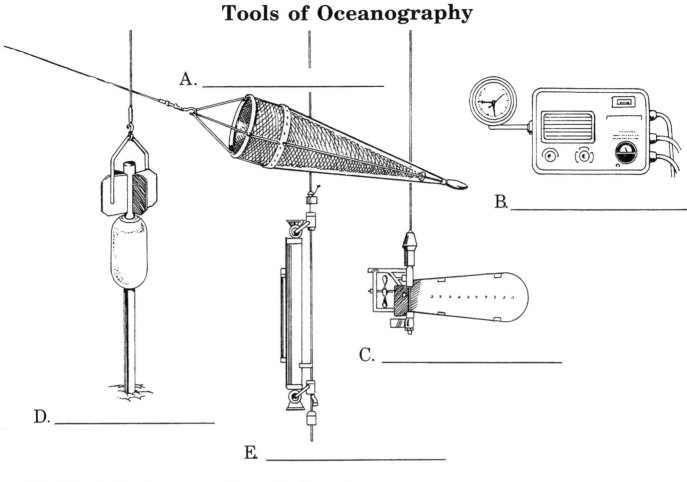

A. _____

B. _____

C. _____

D. _____

E. _____

1. Label the tools of oceanography on the lines above.
2. Circle the tool that traps floating and drifting microscopic plants.
3. Write the word or words that will make each sentence a true statement.

   a. The tool used to get samples below the ocean floor is a _____.

   b. To test the chemical make-up of ocean water, scientists use the _____.

   c. The _____ is used to determine the speed and direction of "rivers" in the ocean.

   d. Echoes are received and recorded on the _____.
4. Write the word or phrase from Column B in the space before its purpose in Column A.

<u>Column A</u>   <u>Column B</u>

_____ a. analyze concentration of sodium sulfate   corer

_____ b. brings up samples of sediments from ocean floor   current meter

_____ c. from 800 meters to 700 meters   water sampler

_____ d. diatoms are gathered and studied   collecting net

_____ e. 1 knot per hour in a westward direction   depth recorder

5. Why is oceanography considered a relatively new science? _____

_____

The Ocean's Storehouse

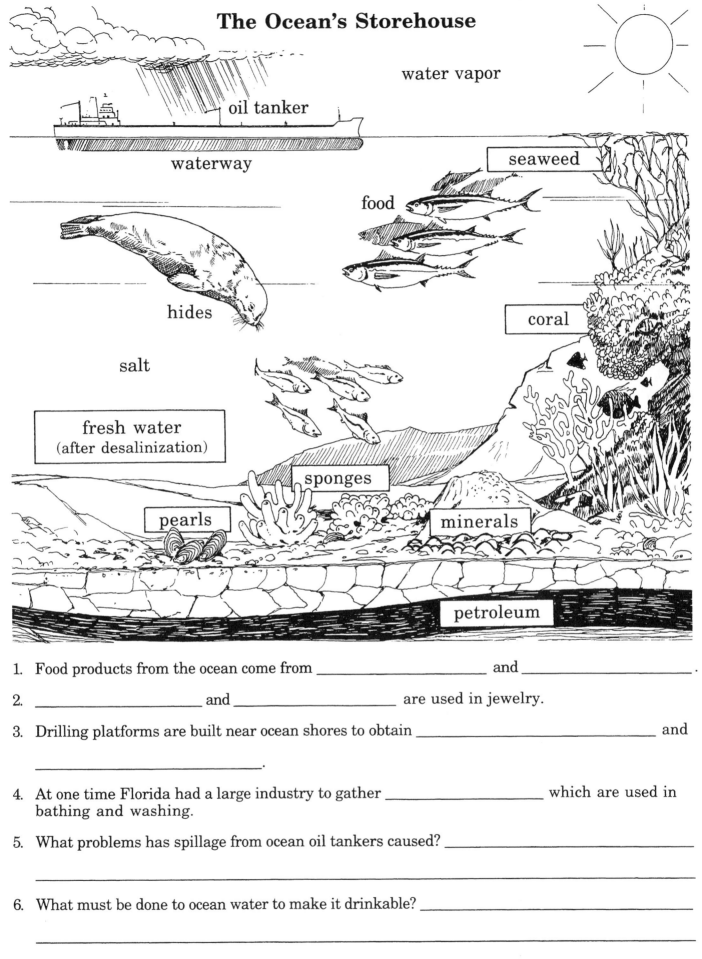

water vapor

oil tanker

waterway

seaweed

food

hides

coral

salt

fresh water
(after desalinization)

sponges

pearls

minerals

petroleum

1. Food products from the ocean come from _____ and _____.

2. _____ and _____ are used in jewelry.

3. Drilling platforms are built near ocean shores to obtain _____ and _____.

4. At one time Florida had a large industry to gather _____ which are used in bathing and washing.

5. What problems has spillage from ocean oil tankers caused? _____

_____

6. What must be done to ocean water to make it drinkable? _____

_____

A Last Look—Part I

A. In each of the following groups one item does not belong. Circle that item and in the space provided explain why it does not belong.

1. North Sea   Gulf of Mexico   Indian Ocean

    _____

2. crest   continental shelf   trough

    _____

3. neon   sodium   chlorine

    _____

4. kelp   algae   fish

    _____

5. corer   stethoscope   depth recorder

    _____

6. air tank   oar   wet suit

    _____

7. Gulf Stream   California Current   Kuroshio Current

    _____

8. flying fish   prawn   viperfish

    _____

9. oil   magnesium   coal

    _____

10. *Alvin*   snorkel   bathyscaphe

    _____

B. Write the word or words that will make each sentence a true statement.

1. The most common mineral matter found in ocean water is _____ .

2. The gravitational pull on the oceans by the _____ and _____
    results in high and low _____ .

3. Two major currents that affect North America are the _____ Current and
    the _____ _____ .

4. The word SCUBA stands for _____ .

5. Microscopic plant and animal life found in ocean water is called _____ .

6. Friction between _____ and _____ produces waves.

7. The three largest oceans of the world are the _____ , _____ ,
    and _____ . Each includes smaller bodies of water called _____ .

8. Due to the lack of _____ , the deep ocean zones are dark with very
    _____ water temperatures.

9. Currents north of the equator flow in a _____ direction.

10. Jellyfish, snails, and crabs are found in _____ water, while
    chiasmodon, sea urchins, and brittle stars are found in _____ water.

A Last Look—Part II

On line A, name the picture. On line B, circle the word or phrase that best applies to line A.

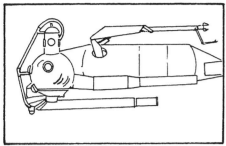

A. _____
B. submersible
   scuba

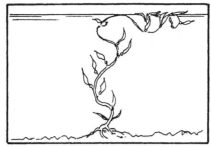

A. _____
B. shallow-water plant
   deep-water plant

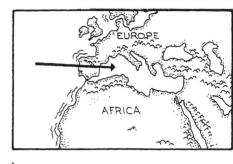

A. _____
B. an ocean
   a sea

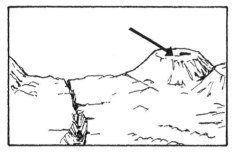

A. _____
B. ocean floor stack
   flat-top volcano

A. _____
B. a "breaker"
   a tsunami

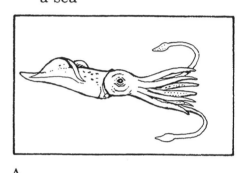

A. _____
B. deep-ocean-zone life
   shallow-ocean-zone life

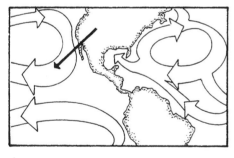

A. _____
B. above-equator current
   below-equator current

A. _____
B. abundant minerals
   abundant plant life

A. _____
B. a marine trench
   a marine rift

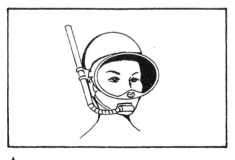

A. _____
B. shallow-water apparatus
   deep-water apparatus

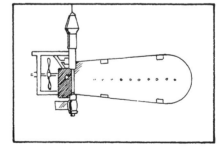

A. _____
B. measures salinity
   measures speed

A. _____
B. free-floating creature
   attached plantlike creature

A Last Look—Part III

A. Find the statement in the second column that best describes each word in the first column. Write the letter of the statement before the word it describes.

1. _____ rift
2. _____ zooplankton
3. _____ Gulf Stream
4. _____ Nansen bottle
5. _____ wavelength
6. _____ sodium chloride
7. _____ kelp
8. _____ ballast
9. _____ squid
10. _____ regulator

a. microscopic animals in the ocean
b. mollusk with tentacles
c. wave with windblown crest
d. type of marine plant
e. current of east coast of U.S.
f. distance between two crests
g. part of an air tank
h. smooth area of ocean floor
i. iron pellets of a submersible
j. water sample collector
k. the mineral salt
l. valley between ridges

B. Circle the word or phrase that will make each sentence a true statement.

1. The observers in a submersible are seated in the _____.

   gondola   ballast   flotation tank

2. Narrow, very deep valleys known as _____ are found in the ocean bottoms.

   ridges   guyots   trenches

3. _____ are giant waves caused by earthquakes.

   Snorkels   Crests   Tsunamis

4. The process of removing salt from ocean water is known as _____

   condensation   desalinization   precipitation

5. The continental land mass that extends about 200 km into the ocean is called the _____.

   continental shelf   continental slope   shoreline

6. The average salinity of ocean water is _____ %.

   .35   5.3   3.5

7. The Humboldt Current is found in the _____ Ocean.

   Atlantic   Pacific   Indian

8. A common animal of shallow ocean water is the _____.

   scallop   kelp   hatchet fish

9. The most important piece of equipment for scuba diving is the _____.

   wet suit   snorkel   air tank

10. The microscopic plant life found near the ocean surface is called _____.

   phytoplankton   coral   sea lettuce

A Last Look—Part IV

A. Explain fully the meaning of this cartoon.

"There doesn't seem to be any fish around here today."

_____

_____

_____

_____

B. There is something wrong with each of these drawings. Circle the part of the drawing that is incorrect and explain why you circled it.

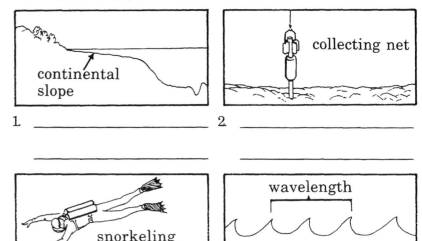

continental slope

collecting net

1. _____

2. _____

_____

_____

snorkeling

wavelength

3. _____

4. _____

_____

_____

C. Write the words that will make each sentence a true statement. Then use these words to complete the fish puzzle.

ACROSS

1. _____ are a favorite seafood.

2. Scallops, clams, and oysters are protected by a _____ .

3. A _____ is a vessel used to explore under the ocean.

4. Red _____ is a common marine plant.

5. Between eastern United States and Europe is the _____ Ocean.

DOWN

1. Air tanks are used in _____ diving.

2. The Caribbean _____ is north of South America.

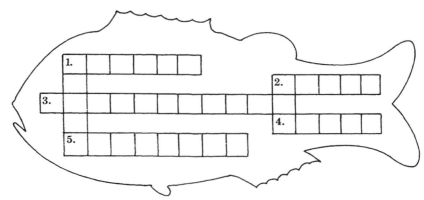

Oceans and Seas of the World

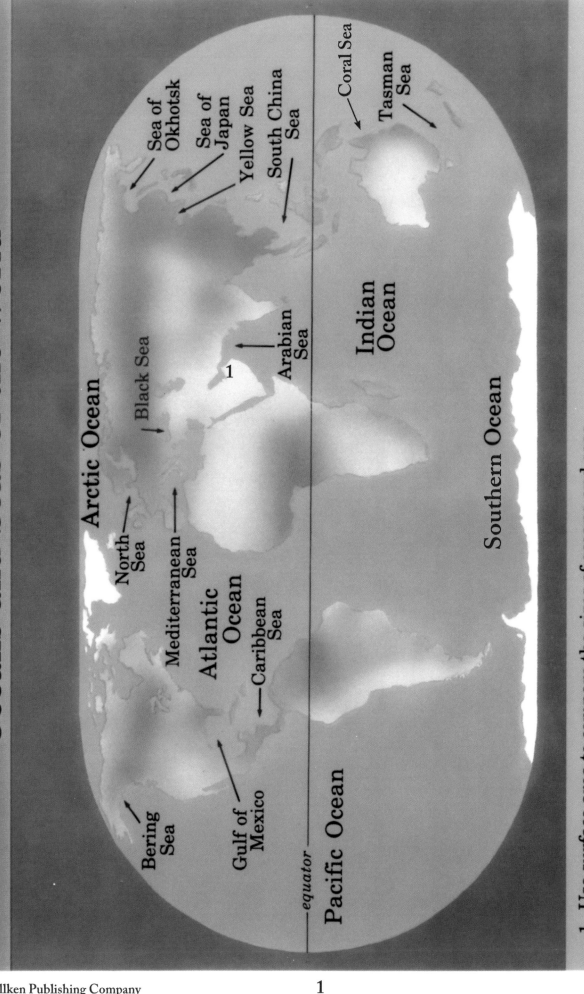

1. Use surface area to compare the sizes of oceans and seas.

2. Why are the separate oceans sometimes referred to as the "world ocean"?

STUDY QUESTION: How do oceans and seas affect the earth's climate?

Major Ocean Currents

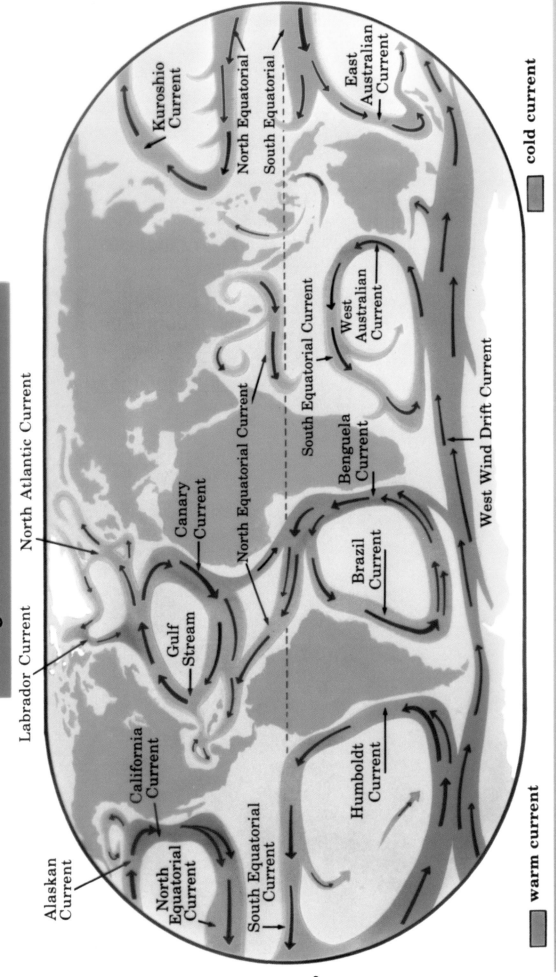

Labrador Current

North Atlantic Current

Alaskan Current

California Current

North Equatorial Current

South Equatorial Current

Gulf Stream

Canary Current

North Equatorial Current

Humboldt Current

Brazil Current

Benguela Current

South Equatorial Current

West Australian Current

West Wind Drift Current

East Australian Current

Kuroshio Current

North Equatorial
South Equatorial

■ warm current

■ cold current

1. Compare the directional flow of currents north of the equator to currents south of the equator.

2. Why are some ocean currents warm and some cold?

STUDY QUESTION: How can a directional change in an ocean current affect marine life?

© Milliken Publishing Company

Oceanography

The Ocean Profile

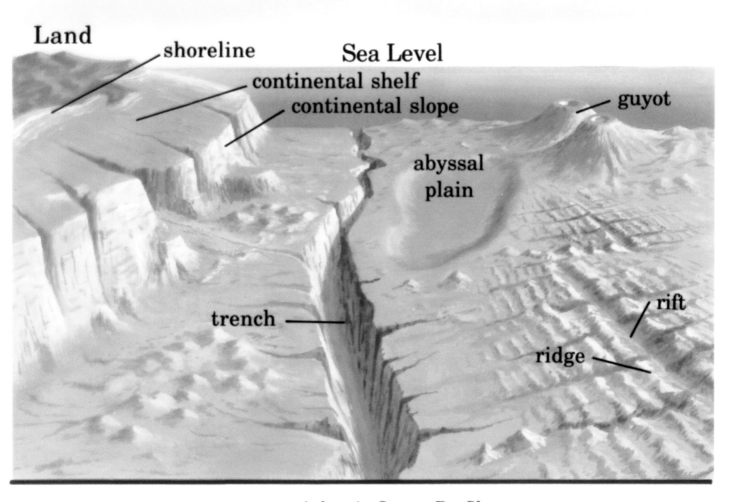

Land

shoreline

Sea Level

continental shelf

continental slope

guyot

abyssal plain

trench

rift

ridge

Atlantic Ocean Profile

Continental Shelf of North America

Continental Shelf of Europe

Meters Sea level

Bermuda Islands

Mid-Atlantic Ridge

1500
3000
4500
6000

1000   2000   3000   4000   5000

Kilometers

1. What is the name of flat-topped underwater mountains?

2. What ocean features have the greatest depth?

STUDY QUESTION: How were ocean depths determined in the early years of exploration?

Waves

Friction between wind and water produces waves.

crest ← wavelength →

height

trough

Whitecaps
Strong wind pushes water off top of wave.

Breakers
Trough hits bottom, crest falls, wave breaks up.

Tsunamis
average speed:
750 kilometers/hour

height:
15-30 meters

1. What giant wave is caused by underwater earthquakes?

2. Define the height of a wave.

STUDY QUESTION: How do water molecules move within a wave?

Characteristics of Ocean Water

Major Elements in Ocean Water

(Element)	(%)
oxygen	} 96.5%
hydrogen	
chlorine	1.9%
sodium	1.1%
magnesium	
sulfur	
calcium..	
potassium	
bromine	
carbon	
iron	0.5%
strontium	
silicon..	
fluorine	
aluminum	
phosphorus...................................	

Common Salts in Ocean Water

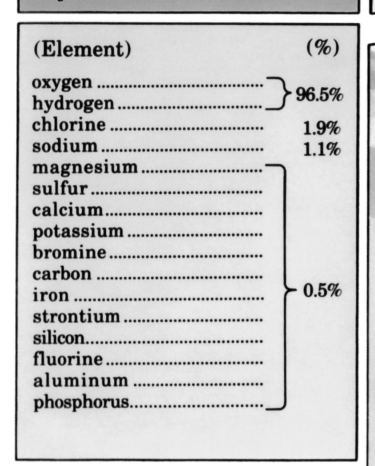

other salt traces (0.1%)
magnesium bromide (0.21%)
calcium carbonate (0.35%)
potassium sulfate (2.46%)
calcium sulfate (3.60%)
magnesium sulfate (4.73%)
magnesium chloride (10.89%)
sodium chloride (77.75%)

- Average salinity of ocean water is 35 parts per 1000 or 3.5%.
- Tropical and some polar ocean waters have above average salinity.

1. Describe some characteristics of ocean water.

2. Why is it not feasible to extract some elements, such as iron and aluminum from ocean water?

STUDY QUESTION: How does Archimedes' Principle explain why a 50,000 ton ocean-going ship, made of iron and steel, floats in ocean waters?

Marine Plant Life

Plant life in ocean waters ranges from microscopic phytoplankton to very large algae.

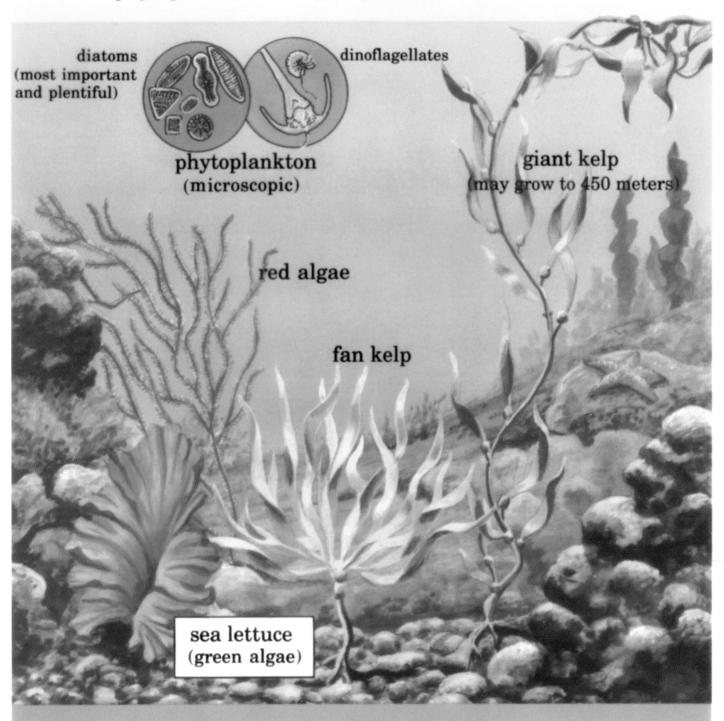

diatoms (most important and plentiful)

dinoflagellates

phytoplankton (microscopic)

giant kelp (may grow to 450 meters)

red algae

fan kelp

sea lettuce (green algae)

1. Describe some of the plant life found in ocean waters.

2. Why does marine animal life depend on marine plant life?

STUDY QUESTION: Find out about the use of algin in foods and other products.

Marine Animal Life: Shallow Water

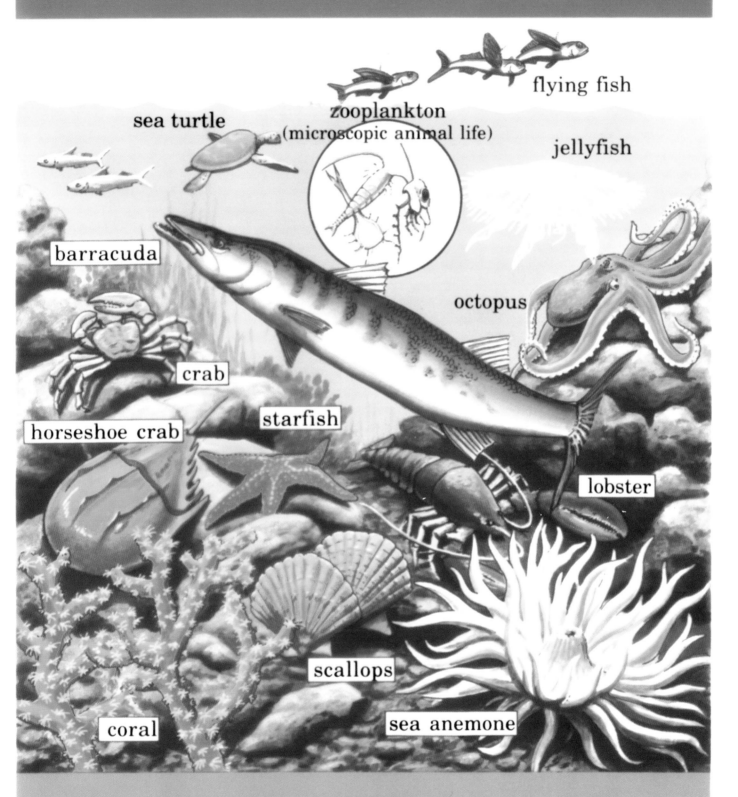

flying fish

sea turtle

zooplankton
(microscopic animal life)

jellyfish

barracuda

octopus

crab

horseshoe crab

starfish

lobster

scallops

coral

sea anemone

1. Describe one food chain seen in this illustration.

2. Which animal is not a true crab but is related to spiders?

STUDY QUESTION: Which animals shown above are classified as
echinoderms, crustaceans, mollusks, fish, reptiles?

Marine Animal Life: Deep Water

prawn

giant squid

hatchet fish

viperfish

chiasmodon

giant tube worm

brittle star

1. Which animal is the likely prey of large toothed-whales?

2. Why are deep-sea organisms not plant feeders?

STUDY QUESTION: What is the source of nutrients for the bacteria around deep-sea geothermal vents?

Submersibles: Deep-Diving Vehicles

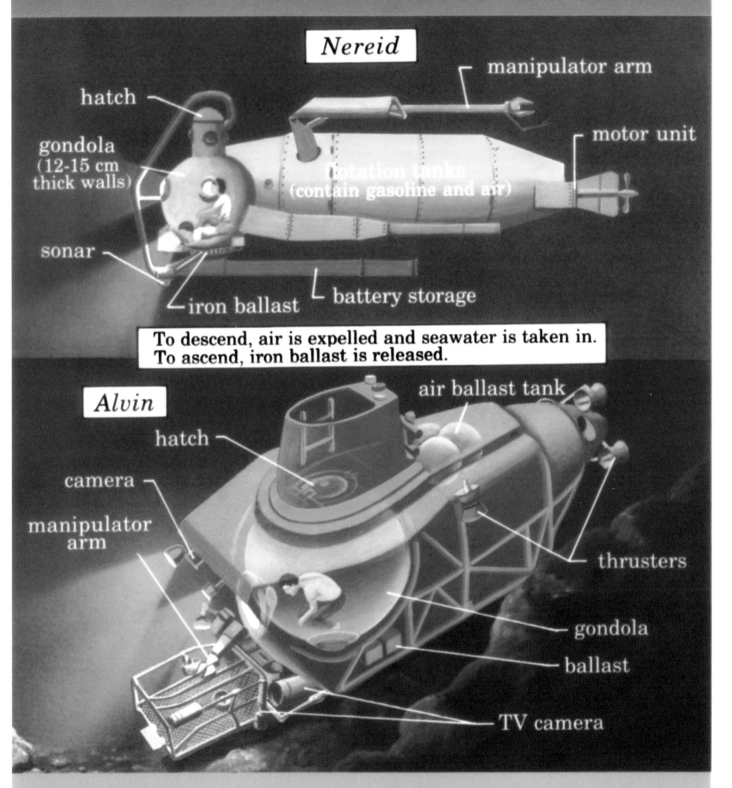

Nereid

hatch

manipulator arm

motor unit

gondola
(12-15 cm
thick walls)

flotation tanks
(contain gasoline and air)

sonar

iron ballast

battery storage

To descend, air is expelled and seawater is taken in.
To ascend, iron ballast is released.

Alvin

air ballast tank

hatch

camera

manipulator
arm

thrusters

gondola

ballast

TV camera

1. What is the source of power for the propulsion motor on a submersible?

2. How are pilots of submersibles able to pick up objects on the ocean floor?

STUDY QUESTION: How were the explorers of the *Titanic*'s ruins able to
film inside the ship?

Snorkeling and Scuba Diving

Snorkeling: average 8-10 meters for 25 seconds

flippers

snorkel

face mask

regulator

air tank

wet suit

face mask

air hose

weight belt

camera

depth gauge

spear gun

fins

Scuba: average 12 m for one hour with one tank

1. Compare the equipment of a scuba diver and a snorkeler.

2. Why can a scuba diver stay longer and go deeper into the ocean than a snorkeler?

STUDY QUESTION: Find out about the invention of Captain Cousteau and Emile Gagnan.

Tools of Oceanography

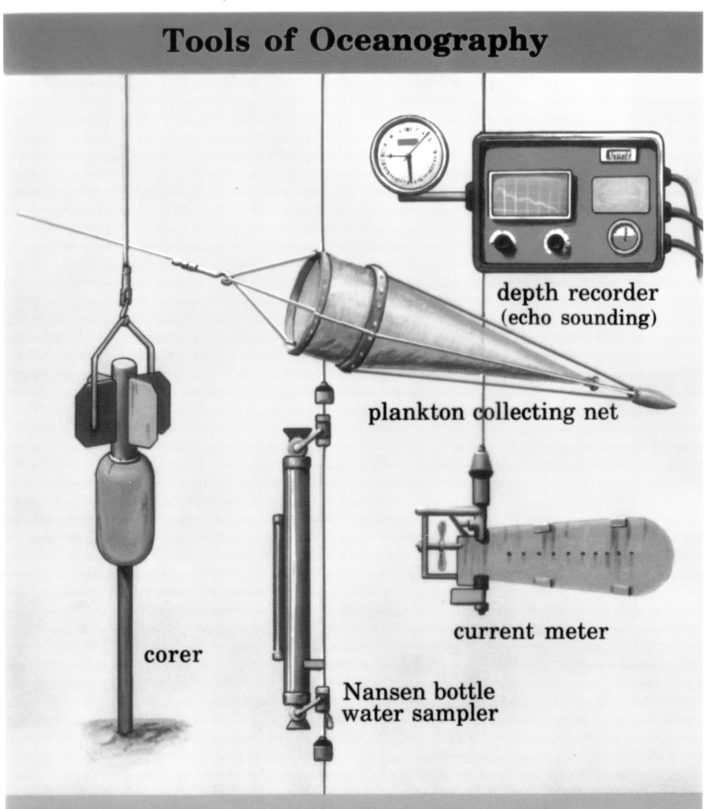

depth recorder
(echo sounding)

plankton collecting net

corer

Nansen bottle
water sampler

current meter

1. List the tools shown above and describe how they are used by
   oceanographers.

2. Why is drilling into the ocean floor important to the oil and gas
   industry?

STUDY QUESTION: Find out about the oceanographic research vessel
FLIP.

The Ocean's Storehouse

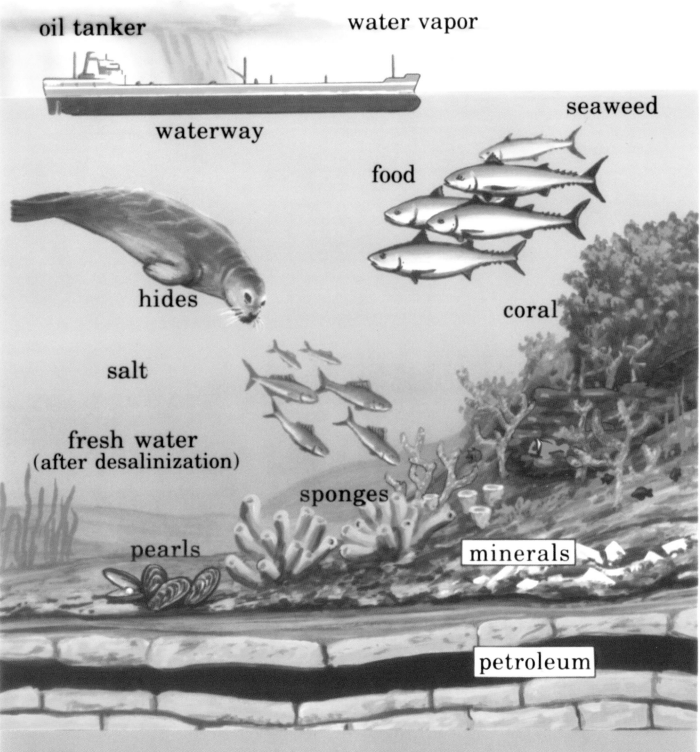

oil tanker

water vapor

waterway

seaweed

food

hides

coral

salt

fresh water
(after desalinization)

sponges

pearls

minerals

petroleum

1. What role does the ocean play in the water cycle?

2. What types of cargo are shipped on ocean waterways?

STUDY QUESTION: Where are deposits of manganese nodules located
and how can they be collected?